EXIT LIKE A BOSS

21 STEP CHALLENGE

DR. CRAIG WEST

Dr. Craig West
Succession Plus Australia Pty Ltd
Level 6, 50 York St
SYDNEY NSW 2000
www.succession.plus

Author Services: https://www.pickawoowoo.com/

First published in 2023.

NATIONAL LIBRARY OF AUSTRALIA

A catalogue record for this book is available from the National Library of Australia.

ISBN: 978-0-9922939-4-9 (paperback)
ISBN: 978-0-9922939-5-6 (e-book)

Disclaimer:

Contents

Step 1 - Introduction and Overview of Exit Strategies

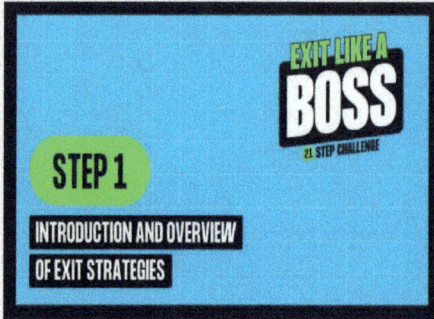

An exit strategy isn't just about selling your business; it's a comprehensive roadmap that defines your business's future, ensuring success for you, your family, your stakeholders, and the legacy you leave behind.

Crafting a robust exit strategy is a fundamental step for any business owner. It provides a clear pathway for the future and ensures that the years you've invested in the business are rewarded, not just financially, but also in terms of legacy and continuity.

Diverse Exit Avenues

Your exit strategy is a multifaceted plan, encompassing various possibilities, such as selling to private equity, going public through an IPO, or transitioning ownership to the next generation. Each exit avenue demands rigorous preparation and strategizing.

As a business owner, you often get consumed in the day-to-day operations, striving to enhance sales, optimize marketing strategies, attract more customers, and elevate profits. However, you might neglect to pause and contemplate the core reason you embarked on this entrepreneurial journey – the problem you aimed to solve.

Critical Aspects of Exit and Succession Planning

Initially, most businesses are created from a desire to address specific problems. Whether it's designing beautiful buildings, fixing plumbing issues, or providing legal solutions, businesses are problem solvers. However, amidst the whirlwind of running a business, the fundamental problem is often overlooked – how to exit the business and extract the value amassed over years, even generations.

Successful exit and succession planning hinge on three critical aspects. First, the business must be primed and ready, with risks managed and preparations in place for ownership and management transitions. Second, the financial aspect, encompassing both business and personal finances, is pivotal. Adequate readiness for retirement or embarking on the next venture is crucial. Finally, your post-business plans play a vital role in a seamless exit.

There are diverse avenues for business exit, such as selling the business, passing it down to the next generation, or exploring options like an IPO, private equity sale, employee share plans, or management buyouts. However, they all require meticulous preparation, and the most successful exits are those with extensive preparation periods.

The Comprehensive 21-Step Exit Strategy

Stage One: Identify Value	STEP 1:	Goals and Outcomes
	STEP 2:	Fact Find
	STEP 3	Business Insights Report
Stage Two: Protect Value	STEP 4:	Financial Planning
	STEP 5:	Unplanned Events
	STEP 6:	De-risking
Stage Three: Maximize Value	STEP 7:	Exit Options
	STEP 8:	Strategic Planning Business Model
	STEP 9:	Strategic Financials
	STEP 10:	Systems and Procedures
	STEP 11:	Marketing and Sales
	STEP 12:	Corporate Governance
	STEP 13:	Ownership Mindset
	STEP 14:	Employee Ownership
	STEP 15:	Management Succession
Stage Four: Extract Value	STEP 16:	Tax Planning
	STEP 17:	Documentation
	STEP 18	Liquidity Event
Stage Five: Manage Value	STEP 19:	Ongoing Investment Planning
	STEP 20:	Asset Protection
	STEP 21:	Estate Planning

In this detailed guide, we present 21 steps across five stages to maximize the value of your business and ensure a successful exit. Each step is carefully crafted to guide you through the complexities of a successful exit, paving the way for a bright future beyond your business.

Remember, preparing for an exit strategy is not just a financial move – it's about ensuring a thriving legacy for your business and securing a prosperous life after business. Here, we will navigate through the stages and steps, unraveling the secrets to successfully exiting like a boss.

Step 2 - Goals and Outcomes

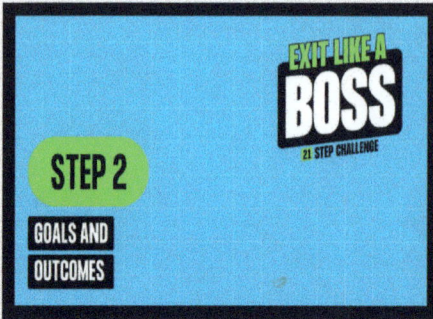

Explore the critical aspects of setting goals and outcomes for your business exit strategy, particularly tailored for SME business owners like yourself. Visualizing a prosperous exit is a vital step in this endeavor. We'll delve into this journey, concentrating on defining goals and desired outcomes for you, your business, your employees, and your financial future.

Clarify Your Business Exit Strategy

Begin with a clear vision of your exit strategy. Many business owners overlook this vital aspect or possess only a vague idea, like selling the business upon reaching a certain age. However, a successful exit demands thorough preparation and clarity in the approach.

Your exit strategy must be specific and time-based. Outline a clear date and envisage the type of buyer, be it a listed company or a private equity fund. Moreover, define the financial aspect of the sale - whether it's a $2 million, $5 million, $10 million, or $50 million deal. Being specific allows you to strategize effectively to achieve your financial goals.

Tailoring Preparation to Your Exit Goals

Preparation varies based on your exit strategy. If you plan to list your company on a stock exchange, certain prerequisites like audited accounts and robust governance systems are necessary. Conversely, passing the business to your children requires structured training and possibly adding specialized roles within the management.

Understanding your intended outcome is crucial in shaping the decision-making and implementation processes throughout the transition.

Plan Your Post-Exit Role and Transition

Clearly define your role post-exit. Decide whether you'll still be actively involved in the business or transition into an advisory or board position. This decision impacts the steps you'll take in the lead-up to the exit.

Consider the expertise needed to support your successor, be it a family member or an external buyer. Plan and implement necessary changes in management and structure to ensure a smooth transition and the ongoing success of the business.

Communicate Your Vision

Effective communication is key. Discuss your exit plans with family members, business partners, and other stakeholders. Keeping everyone informed and aligned with your vision maximizes the likelihood of a successful transition.

Avoid the common mistake of keeping your exit strategy a secret. Sharing your vision and involving others can yield valuable insights and garner support for your journey.

Take Action and Document Your Journey

Document your goals and action plan in a clear, concise manner. Start a journal to record the steps you'll take to achieve a successful exit. Make it a dynamic roadmap that evolves as you progress toward your goals.

In conclusion, setting clear and detailed exit goals is the cornerstone of a successful business exit. By documenting your strategy and involving stakeholders, you set the stage for a smooth transition that maximizes the value of your business.

So, take the next step - sit down, pen your goals, and lay the foundation for an exit that truly embodies exiting like a boss. Your future self and your business will thank you for the foresight and meticulous planning.

Step 3 - Fact Find

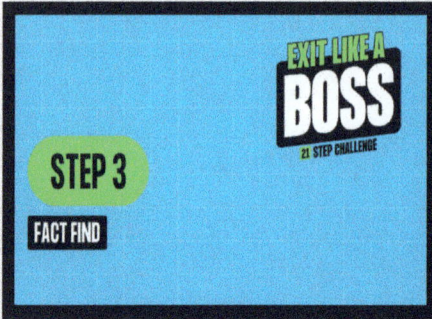

Let's delve into a vital aspect of crafting a solid business exit strategy: the fact-finding mission. Getting to the core of your business operations is the initial stride toward comprehending its actual value and the avenues for expansion. Let's navigate through the pivotal components you must proficiently handle to set the stage for a successful exit.

Understanding Ownership: A Fundamental Step

First and foremost, let's tackle ownership. Your business may have evolved from a simple, singular entity to a complex structure involving various entities, assets, and stakeholders. Understanding the ownership landscape is fundamental, not just for today, but also for the future, especially as you plan for your eventual exit. Consider scenarios where you might sell the business but retain property assets. Each ownership facet has its implications for asset protection and tax considerations.

Analyzing Financial Performance: More Than Just Numbers

Next up is financial performance. This area encompasses more than just the balance sheets. Analyzing your profit and loss statements is vital, but it's equally crucial to adjust for any non-recurring or private expenses.

Benchmarking your financials against industry averages will provide insights into where your business stands in comparison to competitors, influencing potential buyers, investors, or lenders.

Delving into Non-Financial Aspects: Often Overlooked Opportunities

Beyond the financials, delve into the non-financial aspects, an area often overlooked. A comprehensive analysis, akin to our Business Insights Report, involves scrutinizing approximately 300 non-financial factors. These factors tie directly to risk and valuation. Reducing risk elevates your business value, and many of these aspects contribute to mitigating risk. This deep dive helps you identify areas for improvement, potentially increasing the attractiveness of your business to potential buyers.

Gauging Business Valuation: A Key Determinant

Lastly, let's talk about valuation. Accurately gauging your business's current worth is paramount. It's common for business owners to either undervalue or overvalue their enterprises. Understanding your present valuation equips you to chart a course to reach your desired valuation, whether through financial improvements or risk reduction. This may involve a process spanning several months or even years, so starting early is key.

Taking Action: The Road to a Successful Exit

The actionable takeaway here is to gather all the pertinent facts and figures. When you decide to sell, potential buyers will demand a host of documentation for due diligence. Anticipate their needs and prepare accordingly. Complete a comprehensive fact find today, ensuring you have all the critical information readily available for the valuation analysis when the time comes.

Incorporating these practices into your business strategy not only prepares you for a successful exit but also streamlines your business operations and boosts profitability. Stay ahead of the curve by arming yourself with knowledge, making your business a more appealing prospect and securing a prosperous future beyond the exit.

Value Potential

	As of today	Resolve profit gap	Best in Class financials	Foundation (Risk)	Strategic Growth
Revenue	$8,093,000	$8,093,000	$8,093,000	$8,093,000	$8,093,000
EBITDA	$1,615,015	$1,818,852	$1,852,928	$1,852,928	$1,852,928
NOPAT	$1,037,336	$1,192,760	$1,218,743	$1,218,743	$1,218,743
EBITDA Multiple	3.32	3.32	3.32	4.28	4.93
NOPAT Multiple	5.17	5.17	5.17	6.50	7.50
Valuation	$5.36M	$6.16M	$6.30M	$7.92M	$9.14M

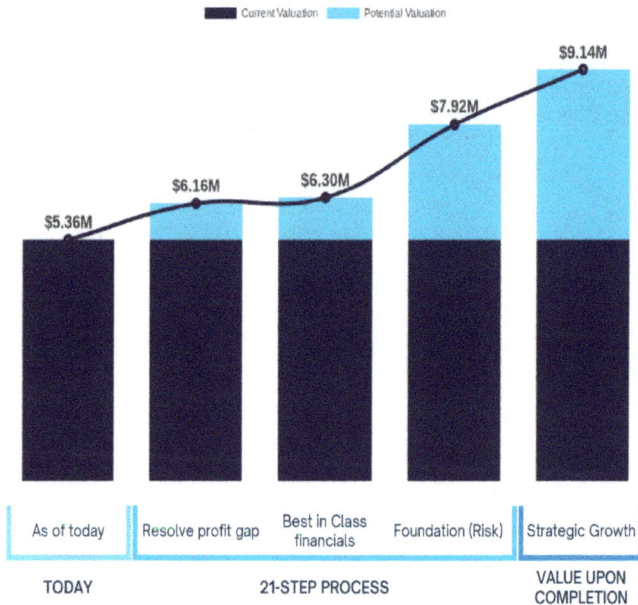

The most important focus should be on value acceleration – the reason our Business Insights Report concludes with a page on value potential is that this is the main game for many owners (even those who are not exiting).

'WHAT IS THE BUSINESS WORTH TODAY?' is only part of the question. **WHAT SHOULD IT OR COULD IT BE WORTH?**

The value potential uses our software algorithm to answer this fundamental question and show what can be done to maximize the value of the business (using the 21-step implementation plan). Closing the profit gap and improving financial performance will increase the value, and then addressing the foundation and strategic growth issues identified will deliver the highest value potential for the business.

Step 4 – Financial Planning

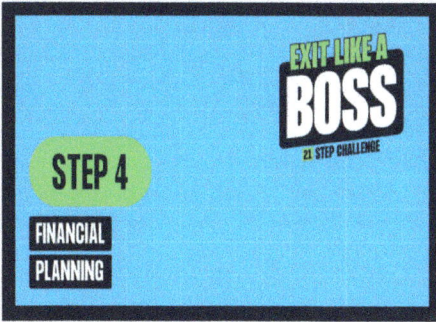

Financial Planning is a pivotal facet in developing your exit strategy. If you're a discerning SME business owner, you may typically connect financial planning with stocks, shares, and investments. Nevertheless, at this juncture, the focus is on strategic foresight for the events leading up to your exit or retirement.

Retirement and Financial Planning

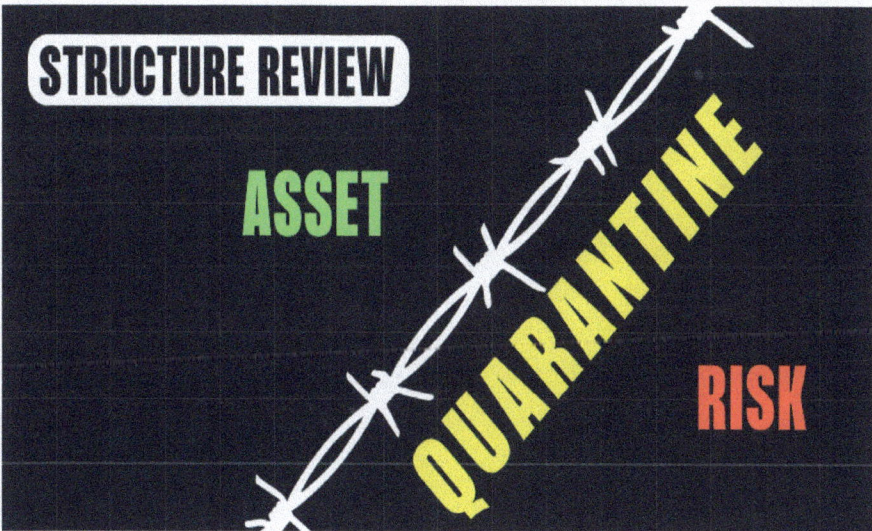

Retirement looms on the horizon, prompting essential questions: How much money do you need to retire comfortably, and where should those funds be invested to ensure protection and optimal growth? Beyond this, you must consider legal safeguards and ownership structures to shield your wealth from potential vulnerabilities tied to the business's sale or unforeseen events.

If retirement isn't your aim and you're eyeing a new venture or business sale, the need for a financial plan is no less crucial. It's about safeguarding and nurturing your wealth, ensuring it aligns with your long-term goals and ambitions post-business exit.

Managing Finances During Business Ownership

In business financials, owners often have the flexibility to infuse personal savings or assets into the company as needed. Dividends and profit shares are commonplace, enabling withdrawals that sustain the owner's financial well-being. However, these dynamics shift once the business is sold, necessitating thorough financial preparation.

To this end, you need a clear financial strategy, identifying asset ownership, protection mechanisms, and tax-efficient structures. The strategic allocation of assets, such as keeping the business intact for sale while leasing the property, can be a shrewd move. However, correct structuring and meticulous ownership tracking are imperative.

Tax-Efficient Structures and Considerations

Your retirement savings, akin to a 401K or a self-managed superannuation fund, should be thoughtfully structured for tax efficiency, accessibility, and security, aligning with a longer, post-retirement life expectancy. Extracting funds from the business in the form of dividends, profit shares, or additional salaries for family members is a prudent step to ensure liquidity outside the business when needed.

Tax implications loom large in business transactions, particularly during a sale. Understanding and leveraging tax concessions for business owners can significantly impact the capital gains tax you incur during the exit. Engaging a financial planner or wealth advisor early on can be invaluable in navigating these tax considerations effectively.

The Collaborative Effort: Building an Advisory Team

Exit planning is a collaborative effort, requiring a well-rounded advisory team. Alongside your CPA and attorney, a financial planner is a vital ally, guiding you through the strategic structuring and planning to ensure you, your family, and stakeholders are prepared for the future.

In conclusion, financial planning for your business exit transcends daily investment choices. It revolves around strategic structuring, protecting assets, and plotting a sustainable course for the next phase of your life – whether that's retirement or a new business endeavor. Seek advice early in this journey to optimize your financial outcome.

Step 5 - Unplanned Events

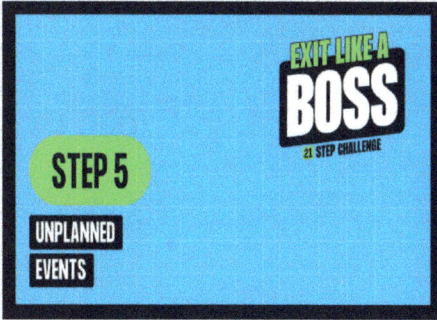

Addressing a crucial but often overlooked topic, we discuss the unexpected occurrences that can severely impact your business's stability and, by extension, your life. What if unforeseen circumstances like a major illness or an accident suddenly strike? How would your business fare in the face of a natural disaster? Preparing for these unforeseen events is essential to safeguard both your business and the well-being of your family.

Safeguarding Your Established Value

Now that we've evaluated the value and potential of our business through a thorough fact-finding mission and a comprehensive Business Insights Report, it's vital to ensure that this value is protected. Unplanned events are an unfortunate reality for many business owners, ranging from minor inconveniences to major disruptions. Hence, we must brace ourselves for what might come our way.

Confronting the reality of unplanned events can be daunting, but with effective planning, their impact can be minimized. As a business owner, your absence due to an unexpected event like a serious illness or accident can have a far-reaching impact. You likely play a key role in the company, being a shareholder, director, and probably an essential employee. Consequently, your absence not only affects the business but also has a significant financial impact on your family.

A Better Way: Buy-Sell Agreements and Insurance

To mitigate the repercussions of such events, many business owners opt for a buy-sell agreement. This legal document transfers the ownership of your shares to other shareholders while ensuring fair compensation for your family or estate. While the legal aspect might be relatively straightforward, funding this arrangement is the real challenge.

Insurance proves to be a viable solution to fund the buy-sell agreement. By insuring your life, you can ensure that your family receives the value of your shares in the event of an unplanned tragedy. This approach provides a structured and stress-free resolution during a challenging time, minimizing disruption not just for your family but also for the business.

The Employee Aspect: Key Person Insurance

Furthermore, if you are a crucial part of the business, like the CEO or a major revenue generator, your absence can also impact the business. Key person insurance steps in to provide financial support to the business, aiding in finding a replacement and mitigating the downturn in sales due to the disruption caused.

Unplanned events are precisely that - unplanned. However, this lack of predictability should not deter you from preparing for the potential fallout. Assess the value of your business and contemplate the possible unplanned events that could occur. If your business heavily relies on you, it's imperative to take action and create a strategy to minimize the risks associated with such events.

Your Action Plan

The key takeaway from this discussion is to take proactive steps to secure the future of your business. Seek guidance from professionals in legal matters, financial planning, and insurance to ensure you have the necessary strategies and documentation in place to mitigate these risks. Safeguarding the value of your business on the path to a successful future is a crucial goal.

Prepare for the unexpected, plan for the future, and ensure that your business continues to thrive regardless of the challenges that come your way.

Step 6 - De-risking

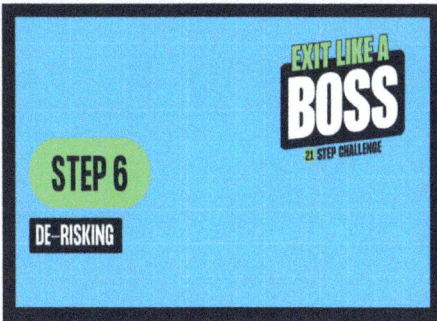

We'll thoroughly explore the essential yet frequently underestimated element of mitigating risk in your business. While it may not be the most thrilling subject, its significance in determining your business's value cannot be overstated. Our goal is to provide insight into the often-neglected aspect of the valuation equation – profit and risk.

Risks and Business Valuation

As a savvy SME business owner, you're undoubtedly aware that the risks your business faces - whether it's the potential of business failure, fluctuating profits, unplanned events, or day-to-day operations – all contribute to a risk score, influencing the valuation. The higher the risk, the lower the valuation. This holds especially true for privately owned businesses.

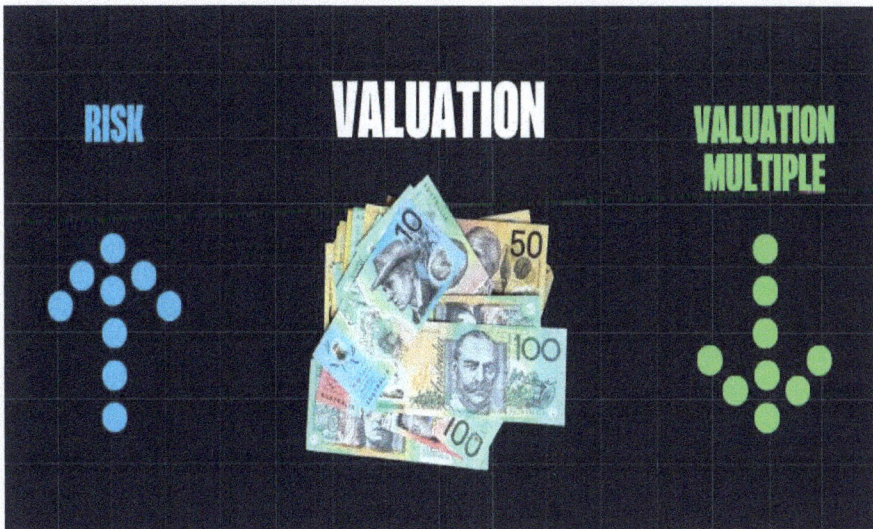

So, how can you effectively de-risk your business and bolster its valuation? The first step is to comprehend the plethora of risks your business might encounter. These risks vary in severity, with some posing minor concerns while others could potentially lead to a catastrophic failure. To get started, compile a comprehensive list of these risks that could affect your business.

Assessing and Scoring Risks

Consider risks such as a delivery driver experiencing a flat tire during a crucial delivery or a driver delivering seafood to a restaurant without proper refrigeration, potentially causing food poisoning. Assess each risk based on two vital aspects: the likelihood of the risk occurring and the seriousness or implications if it does occur.

Combining the likelihood and seriousness of these risks provides a risk score. Lower likelihood and lower severity result in a lower risk score, while higher likelihood and severity lead to a higher score. Focus on addressing the risks with higher scores, working to minimize their occurrence and impact.

Developing simple checklists, templates, policies, and procedures tailored to each area of your business can be instrumental in minimizing risks. For instance, implementing a pre-trip checklist for drivers to ensure the vehicle's safety and functionality can mitigate potential delivery mishaps.

Proactive Risk Management for Enhanced Valuation

Extend this approach to various aspects of your business, such as IT and cybersecurity, financial management, and payment processes. Align your efforts with the aim of minimizing risks throughout your operations.

Remember, a prospective buyer conducting due diligence on your business will thoroughly examine its operational performance and risk management. Taking proactive steps to identify, evaluate, and mitigate risks not only enhances the safety and stability of your business but also increases its valuation potential.

In conclusion, embarking on a risk review and strategically addressing these risks can significantly de-risk your business and maximize its valuation. Start by tackling the more substantial risks, implementing necessary measures, and watch as your business becomes more appealing to potential buyers. Minimizing risk is key to exiting your business like a boss and achieving optimal valuation.

Step 7 - Exit Options

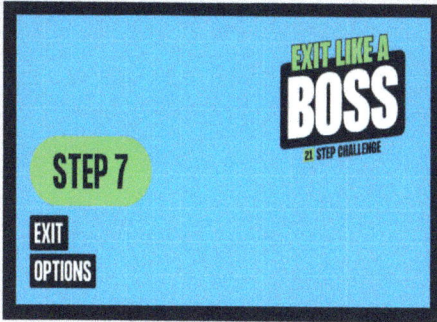

If you are a business owner contemplating the diverse range of exit options available for your venture, with around 15 to 20 potential routes to exit your business, it's crucial to understand which of these are the most suitable and advantageous for you.

Understanding the Range of Exit Options

Here, we'll delve into the most relevant exit strategies. These strategies exist on a spectrum, varying in complexity, cost, speed of implementation, and associated risks.

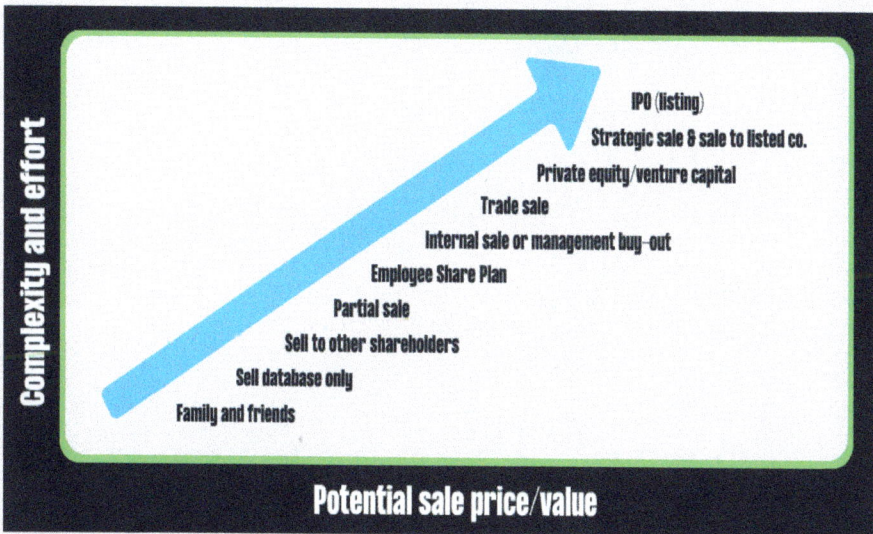

Transferring to Family and Friends

Starting at the simpler end of the spectrum, transferring your business to family, friends, or close associates is a quick and easy exit option. While it may not yield the highest financial returns, it involves minimal risk and associated costs.

IPO: The Pinnacle of Exit Strategies

At the more intricate end of the spectrum is listing your company on a public stock exchange through an IPO. Although it offers the highest financial return, this route is time-consuming, costly, and comes with inherent market risks.

Exploring Mid-Spectrum Options for Private Businesses

In the middle of the spectrum are several options tailored to private businesses, providing a balance of complexity and suitability for businesses not suited for a public listing or family transfer.

Strategic Approaches for Maximizing Value

Consider combining multiple exit strategies sequentially to maximize value at each step of the process. For instance, beginning with a management buy-in or employee share plan to secure key personnel, then partnering with a private equity firm to foster growth before ultimately selling the business to a listed company.

Understanding the fundamental drivers behind these exit strategies is vital. The dichotomy between financial harvest strategies and legacy or stewardship strategies defines the essence of your exit. Many business owners, particularly from the baby boomer generation, are increasingly considering a balanced approach, affording financial gains while ensuring the preservation of the business's legacy.

Setting Goals for Your Exit Strategy

The importance of setting clear goals and outcomes for your exit strategy cannot be overstated. Your chosen strategy profoundly impacts your decision-making throughout the business journey, influencing hiring choices, organizational structure, and resource allocation.

In conclusion, your exit strategy is not merely an endpoint - it's a compass that guides your business decisions. Understanding your desired exit option, whether it's a financial harvest or a legacy-focused approach, empowers you to steer your business towards a prosperous and meaningful future. Gear up to exit like a boss, knowing that your strategy aligns with your vision and values, paving the way for a successful transition.

Step 8 - Strategy and Business Model

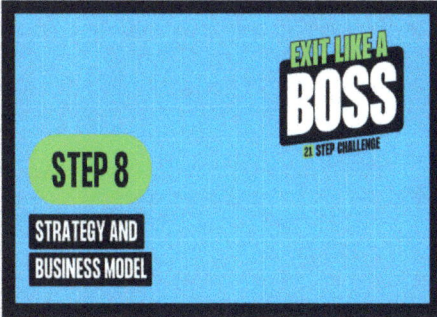

Embarking on a journey toward a successful exit for your SME business requires careful navigation through the realms of strategic planning and business model development. As an astute business owner, the ultimate goal is a successful exit, but achieving that vision hinges on a seamless alignment of your strategic objectives and your chosen business model. Here, we will dissect the essential components of this alignment process, guiding you on the path to creating a well-tailored business plan that harmonizes with your exit strategy.

Setting Clear Goals

In the early stages of the process, you've set your exit goals – let's say selling your business for a significant sum, like $10 million, to a listed company. Now, to accomplish this goal, you need to translate it into tangible financial targets. In this example, aiming for five times multiple on a net profit of $2 million annually is a conservative estimate. This financial foundation provides a roadmap for your strategic planning and business model.

Tailoring Your Business Model

Your business model should align with your financial target. One critical consideration is whether your business is a boutique model or a scale model. A boutique business, such as a high-end restaurant like Rockpool, thrives on a premium-based model – delivering high service, exclusive menus, and a premium price. On the other end of the spectrum is the scale model, characterized by high volume, efficiency, and a focus on speed, like the McDonald's approach.

Avoiding the Middle Ground

Here's the key: avoid the middle ground. Many businesses make the mistake of trying to cater to both ends of the scale simultaneously. For example, attempting to provide both volume-based services and boutique offerings can create confusion, lead to inconsistent pricing, and compromise service quality. Instead, choose one end of the spectrum that aligns with your business and focus on excelling in that area.

The further you position your business towards either extreme, the more likely you are to excel and stand out from competitors. Your business model, services, pricing, and employee skill sets should harmonize with your chosen path. For instance, if you're aiming for a $2 million net profit, determine the volume and pricing that aligns with your model. If you're a scale business, like McDonald's, you need to understand how many units you need to sell daily and what staffing and operational structures are required to achieve this goal.

Executing Your Business Plan

To exit like a boss, ensure your business plan is intricately woven into your chosen business model. Every aspect, from the people you employ to your pricing strategy, needs to align with your overarching goals. Businesses that master this alignment tend to succeed, while those stuck in the middle struggle to gain traction and clarity. It's crucial to be deliberate and focused, embracing either the boutique or scale model and tailoring your business plan accordingly.

As an SME business owner with a keen eye on a successful exit, the key lies in meticulous strategic planning and a well-aligned business model. Embrace the concept of either being a boutique or scale business and structure your business plan accordingly. The clearer your direction and adherence to your chosen model, the smoother your path towards a successful exit will be. Don't get caught in the middle – exit like a boss by choosing the right path and executing your plan flawlessly.

Step 9 - Strategic Financials

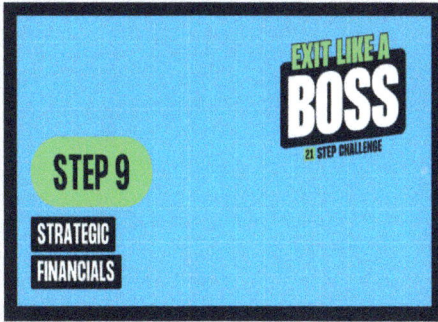

When it comes to business exit strategies, understanding your financials is not just about planning for you, the shareholders, or your family - it's about strategic financial planning for your business. In this discussion, we will explore the vital aspects of strategic financial planning, focusing on achieving your desired business exit outcome.

The Gap: Planning for the Desired Outcome

Let's start with a scenario: imagine your business has opted to sell to a listed company for $10 million, requiring a net profit of approximately $2 million. Achieving this multiple from the listed company is undoubtedly appealing, but it requires meticulous planning. Merely hoping to reach $2 million net profit by some future exit date isn't a viable strategy. A well-defined financial plan is essential.

The first step is planning your financials year on year. However, this isn't about adding a percentage to last year's profit and projecting it as the next year's budget. Instead, it's a detailed evaluation of your current financial performance, considering turnover, gross profit margin, overhead costs, and net profit.

Let's assume you're currently turning over $5 million and making a net profit of $1 million. If your goal is to achieve a net profit of $2 million within 10 years for a successful exit, you need to increase your net profit by at least $100,000 annually.

Simplified Strategic Financial Budgets

Rather than getting lost in intricate calculations, focus on a high-level budget outlining the desired profit outcome. Consider aspects like turnover targets and gross profit margins. Determine the number of units to sell, staffing requirements, and associated costs. Keep it simple, covering the critical elements of your financial strategy.

Ensure that the growth rate you plan for is sustainable and feasible. Can you fund the projected growth to meet your exit goals? If not, adjustments in your plans or securing additional funding may be necessary.

Your strategic financial planning should align with your business model, chosen exit strategy, and overall goals. The financial model should mirror the value potential of your business, making sure every step leads you towards achieving your exit goal.

Avoiding Unpleasant Surprises

A well-structured financial plan ensures there are no unpleasant surprises. It guarantees that you won't reach your exit date and realize that the financials didn't add up, potentially impacting the value of your business in the market.

Strategic financial planning is an essential component of your business exit strategy. It's about ensuring your financial goals match your desired business outcomes. By aligning your financials with your business model and chosen exit strategy, you increase the certainty of achieving your exit goals and exiting like a true boss. So, delve into your financials, plan strategically, and make your exit a successful reality.

Step 10 - Systems and Procedures

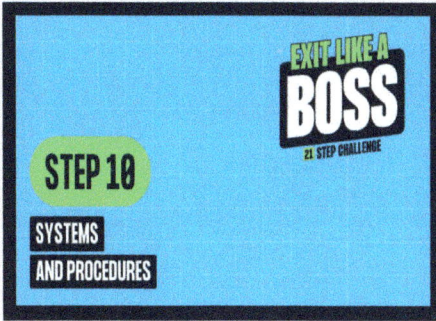

We get it – discussing systems, policies, and procedures might not make your heart race with excitement. However, in this journey of Exit Like a Boss, we're looking at a critical aspect that can significantly impact how potential buyers, lenders, or investors perceive your business. The focus here is to transform your business into an organized, efficient entity – a truly attractive prospect.

The Evolution of Businesses

Many businesses evolve over time, starting small with a couple of owners or founders and eventually growing in size and complexity. As your business expands, the processes that initially worked may become outdated or inadequate for the larger scale of operations. You start noticing variations in how different offices or branches handle tasks. This is where inefficiencies creep in, jeopardizing the streamlined functioning of your business.

Streamlining your business operations through well-defined systems, policies, and procedures is paramount. It's about ensuring everyone in your team knows exactly what to do and how to do it. Not only does this enhance efficiency, but it also minimizes risks by ensuring compliance with established processes.

From a buyer's perspective, this all boils down to risk assessment. Any deviation from established processes introduces risk into the business. Imagine having different methods for making a simple burger – it slows down operations, increases costs, and introduces inconsistency. Just like in a busy kitchen, your business needs a standardized set of instructions and processes to function smoothly and efficiently.

Implementing a Systemized Approach

Look at industry leaders like McDonald's; they have mastered the art of systemization. Every step of their operations is meticulously planned and timed for optimal efficiency. Similarly, in your business, every action, from handling a client request to managing product variations, should follow a standardized process. Modern technology offers countless tools to document and systemize these processes.

One of the keys to success is documenting your policies and procedures in an accessible and user-friendly manner. A well-documented system empowers your team to act confidently and efficiently in any scenario, regardless of their role or experience level.

An efficiently systemized business doesn't just function smoothly; it becomes less reliant on any single individual, including you. It's a show of consistency, reliability, and professionalism to both your internal team and your customers. Moreover, it Saves YourSelf Time, Effort, and Money – the true essence of systems.

Regardless of your business's nature, consider systemizing everything. Implement policies and procedures, leverage technology, and showcase a business that's structured, disciplined, and ready for success. By minimizing risk, maximizing efficiency, and ensuring consistency, your business becomes incredibly appealing to potential buyers, lenders, and investors.

In conclusion, embrace the power of systems, policies, and procedures as you pave your way to exit like a true boss. Your journey toward efficiency and streamlining isn't just about impressing others; it's about shaping a better, more lucrative future for your business. Start systemizing, start adding value, and start exiting with confidence.

Step 11 – Marketing and Sales

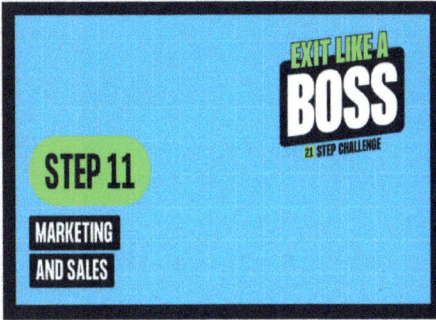

As an SME business owner, you're likely considering how to elevate your business's value and ensure a seamless transition when the time comes for an exit. Here, we'll cover the critical aspects of marketing and sales within the context of devising a strategic exit plan.

One of the foremost considerations in this strategy is ensuring that your marketing and sales efforts are not solely reliant on you as the business owner. Over-dependence on personal interactions and relationships can pose significant challenges when transitioning out of your business. Imagine a scenario where a significant portion of your clientele is tied to your personal networking efforts. When you step back or exit, these clients may no longer remain loyal to the business.

To mitigate this risk, two fundamental components need to be in place: a robust marketing funnel and an effective sales capability.

Marketing Funnel: The Path to a Continuous Stream of Leads

Building a marketing funnel involves establishing an online presence through a website, social media, and digital marketing. The goal is to automate lead generation processes to consistently attract potential customers without your direct involvement. While setting up this system requires initial effort and investment, the long-term benefits are significant.

For instance, utilizing tools like HubSpot, your website can become a hub where visitors can access valuable resources such as whitepapers, eBooks, webinars, or podcasts. By enticing them to fill out forms or provide their details to access these resources, they become part of your marketing funnel.

Sales Capability: Beyond You, the Owner

Your sales process needs to be streamlined and not centered around you. This can be achieved through various means, from e-commerce platforms for online sales to a well-structured sales team that handles client interactions.

In certain businesses, implementing scripts for sales interactions can be highly effective. These scripts guide sales personnel in using key phrases and strategies that resonate well with potential customers, increasing the likelihood of successful conversions.

The Intersection of Marketing, Sales, and Business Strategy

The synchronization of marketing and sales with your business model and strategic financial plan is pivotal. If your goal is to sell the business for a specific amount in the future, your sales plan should be designed to attain that goal. Reverse engineering from the target revenue, understanding conversion rates, and identifying the sources of leads provide a structured pathway towards achieving the desired outcomes.

Regularly evaluating your marketing and sales strategies is vital to ensure their effectiveness. Calculate the return on investment (ROI) for various marketing channels and continually refresh your campaigns to stay relevant and engaging.

In summary, building a strong marketing funnel, developing a sales capability independent of the owner, and aligning these aspects with your business strategy are key steps towards securing your business's value and facilitating a smooth exit process. By doing so, you enhance the potential for generating consistent revenue even after your departure, a crucial factor in exiting like a boss.

Through meticulous planning and strategic execution, you can position your business to thrive beyond your ownership, making it an attractive proposition for potential buyers or successors. Take charge of your marketing and sales strategy today and pave the way for a successful exit in the future.

Step 12 - Corporate Governance

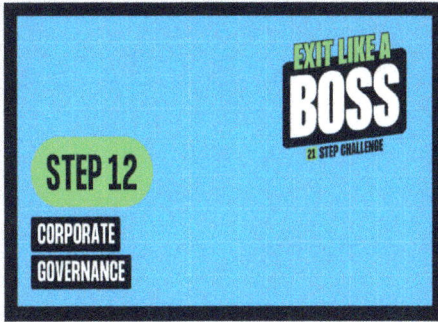

Let's discuss corporate governance – a term that's often misconstrued, particularly by small to medium-sized business owners. While the level of formality may vary for smaller businesses, the principles of structure and discipline that corporate governance brings are crucial, regardless of your business size.

In the early stages, your family-owned or small business might manifest corporate governance in informal dinner discussions involving business matters. However, as your business grows, so does the necessity for a more structured approach. Let's talk about how you can implement an effective corporate governance system, tailored to your business's unique needs and size.

Foundations of Corporate Governance

In the infancy of your business, consider establishing an advisory board comprising trusted advisors – a step that many small businesses take. This advisory board should convene regularly to discuss critical business matters, much like a board meeting in a larger corporation. The key is to focus on gaining insights, strategic planning, and effective decision-making.

Structured Reporting

Reports are the backbone of effective corporate governance. These reports should cover various aspects of your business, including financials, HR, sales, and marketing. By reviewing these reports before meetings, both you and your team can make the right decisions that align with your overall business strategy. Remember, it's about strategic insights, not micromanagement.

Strategic Focus and Discipline

Corporate governance should shift your focus from day-to-day operations to a strategic overview of your business. It's about identifying weaknesses, optimizing performance, and aligning actions with your long-term business goals. This strategic shift is pivotal to successful corporate governance.

Assembling the Right Advisory Board or Directors

As your business grows, consider incorporating independent directors with diverse expertise. These individuals, external to the day-to-day operations, provide a fresh perspective, challenge decisions, and mentor your team. They bring structure, strategy, and an invaluable reduction in business risks.

Decision Rights Manual: Defining Authority

Implement a decision rights manual to outline who holds decision-making authority at various levels within your business. This simple yet effective tool ensures that decisions align with expertise and responsibility levels, mitigating costly errors and promoting agility in decision-making.

Enhancing Value and Reducing Risk

By integrating structure and discipline through corporate governance, you inherently reduce risks and increase the value of your business. Potential buyers or investors find businesses with robust corporate governance systems more attractive due to their decreased risk profile and well-defined operational strategies.

Corporate governance isn't just for large corporations – it's a strategic tool that can significantly impact SMEs. Through the implementation of structured reporting, strategic focus, and the right advisory board or directors, you're laying a strong foundation for the future of your business.

Step 13 – Ownership Mindset

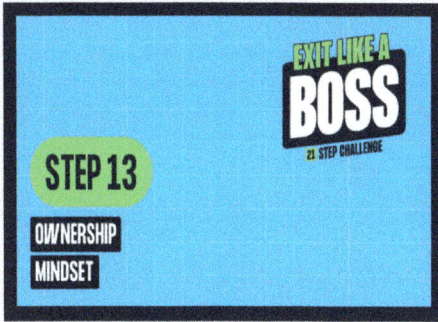

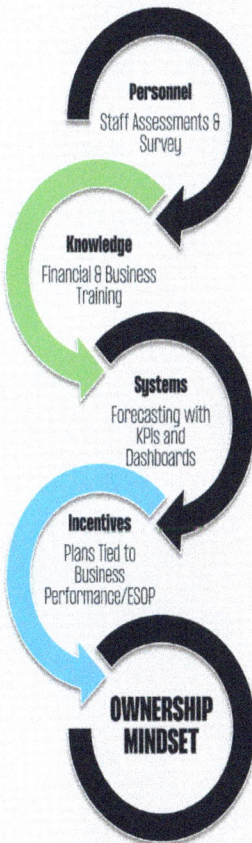

Imagine the impact on your organization if every team member approached their role with the same dedication and strategic thinking as a business owner. It's not just a utopian vision - it's an achievable reality, and employees tend to genuinely enjoy this perspective shift.

The Vision: Employee as a Business Owner

Most employees want to excel in their roles and contribute to a successful company. They yearn to look back at their week and feel a sense of accomplishment, knowing they've met targets and delivered outstanding outcomes. However, many employees lack the necessary tools and understanding to think and act like business owners. They were initially hired for their specific expertise - be it in air conditioning maintenance or any other field - not for their entrepreneurial skills.

Equipping Your Team: The Essential Tools

To instill an ownership mindset within your team, it starts with education. Ensuring you have the right people in the right positions is crucial. Next, it's vital to educate them about the critical factors that drive the success of their role and the business as a whole. This might involve enlightening them about key performance indicators (KPIs), leading indicators, and the financial aspects of your enterprise that impact its success.

In a professional services firm, this education could revolve around billable percentages, time-based billing, and how their individual efforts contribute to the business's financial health. For an air conditioning maintenance team, it could mean understanding the components that drive profitability and efficiency in their operations.

Tapping into Employee Insights: Maximizing Potential

In addition to education, involving your employees in identifying areas of inefficiency and wastage within the business is invaluable. Employees often possess keen insights into daily operations and customer interactions, making them a rich source of actionable suggestions for improving processes and reducing unnecessary expenses. Creating an environment where employees feel comfortable providing feedback and ideas can lead to remarkable improvements.

Incentivizing Proactive Behavior: The Power of Rewards

Creating a well-structured incentive plan is crucial. This plan should reward the desired behavioral changes that align with the business's goals. Choosing appropriate KPIs and matching them with suitable incentives is key to encouraging employees to go the extra mile and think proactively about their roles and the business's success.

Fostering an ownership mindset among your employees involves assembling the right team, providing them with the right education and tools, and incentivizing the right behavior. Employees are more than just the tasks they perform - they are potential partners in growing and improving your business. By empowering them to think and act like business owners, you not only enhance their engagement and satisfaction but also boost your business's value and set the stage for a successful exit strategy.

Step 14 - Employee Ownership

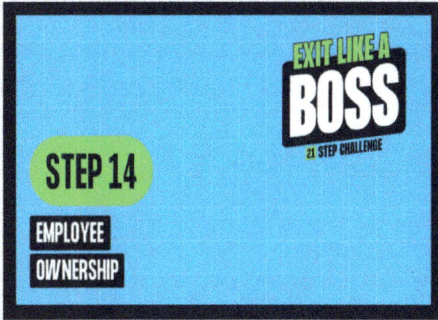

Let's look beyond theoretical concepts and into actionable steps, focusing on cultivating an ownership mindset among employees. More than a mere theory, we advocate for a tangible sense of ownership that translates into meaningful actions.

The Core of Employee Ownership: A Psychological Shift

Employee share plans are a prevalent means of achieving this, although the approaches can vary. The crucial focus here is on understanding the psychology of ownership and its transformational potential, rather than getting lost in legal or financial structures. We're talking about instilling a genuine sense of ownership in employees and all the associated benefits.

Shifting Dynamics: From Employee to Co-Owner

The fundamental shift in this scenario is the transformation of the relationship dynamic within the organization. When employees hold equity in the business, whether through shares or employee share plans, the traditional divide between employee and owner dissipates. Suddenly, we're all co-owners, sharing in the prosperity of the business. The success of the business now directly impacts each member's equity value, aligning us all toward a common goal: enhancing the business's value for mutual financial gain.

The Financial Advantage: Equity and Beyond

Moreover, having a tangible stake alters the financial landscape for employees. They get to experience the dual benefit of an increased business value and a share in the company's profits through dividends. This dynamic not only enhances individual prosperity but also fosters a shared commitment to the growth and success of the enterprise.

Regardless of the ownership model adopted, the ultimate goal remains a triple win scenario. Employees are empowered, gaining a sense of ownership and reaping tangible benefits, such as building equity and receiving dividends - transforming their relationship with the workplace. Founders and existing shareholders also benefit, despite relinquishing a portion of their ownership. Often, the overall value of their retained equity appreciates, mitigating risks associated with employee turnover.

Advantages for the Business: Stability and Attraction

The business itself experiences significant advantages. Employee turnover, a significant risk in many businesses, is substantially reduced. A business with committed and incentivized employees becomes a more attractive prospect for potential buyers or investors. Employee ownership is about securing the future of the business and fostering a culture of loyalty and dedication among employees.

Strategies for Implementation: Partial or Complete Ownership Transfer

In some cases, businesses opt to sell a portion of the company to employees, gradually transitioning ownership. This strategic move serves as an exit plan, with employees gradually taking over the reins. It's a testament to the viability of employee ownership as a long-term business strategy, not merely an exit tactic.

Employee ownership can also be a vital component of succession planning, especially in family businesses where the next generation might not be stepping into the family role. By bringing in non-family employees as partial owners, the business ensures alignment of interests and motivates them to protect and grow the business - bridging the gap between family ownership and a new era.

Empowering the Workforce: Beyond Financial Gains

Lastly, beyond the financial benefits, employee ownership empowers the workforce. Educating them about ownership and providing avenues to acquire equity instills a sense of responsibility and commitment. Dispelling myths about employee preferences for ownership and creatively structuring ownership acquisition mechanisms can make this a viable and attractive option for all parties involved.

In conclusion, incorporating employee ownership into your business strategy can be a game-changer. It's not just about an exit strategy; it's about instilling a sense of shared ownership, driving growth, and ensuring a prosperous future for both the business and its dedicated workforce.

Step 15 – Management Succession

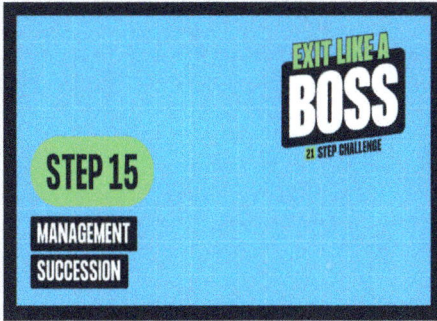

For any small and medium-sized business (SME) owner eyeing an exit strategy, management succession holds a pivotal aspect. It's not just about who owns the business - it's about who will run it effectively. Often, this crucial aspect is overlooked amidst the broader discussions of ownership succession.

Mapping the Organization: Understanding Roles and Growth

The first step in navigating the terrain of management succession is understanding your organizational chart. Who are the key players, and what roles do they currently embody? What are their experiences, qualifications, and duration with your company? This assessment provides a foundation to envision the future.

Peering into the crystal ball of your business's growth, you need to foresee what roles will be essential in 12 months, 2 years, and 5 years. As your business expands, new positions and responsibilities will emerge. For instance, an internal bookkeeper might need to evolve into a CFO. This transformation necessitates a strategic approach - either upskilling the existing talent or recruiting externally.

Designing a Succession Roadmap: Crafting Future Leaders

A critical aspect of management succession involves designing a roadmap for potential successors. Whether it's for a CFO role or any other key position, detailing the necessary skills, qualifications, and experiences is fundamental. Moreover, a clear succession plan should outline the steps employees need to take over the coming years to seamlessly transition into these critical roles.

Incorporating a management succession plan isn't just a strategic move for the business; it's a boon for employees too. Most employees aspire to advance in their careers, to take on more responsibilities, and to enhance their earnings. By providing a clear progression plan, you not only boost employee satisfaction but also retain valuable talent.

The End Goal: Reducing Dependency on the Owner

Perhaps the most critical aspect of management succession is to reduce the business's dependency on the owner. Businesses where everything relies on a single person - be it for product design, client relationships, or financial decisions - often face significant challenges when it comes to valuation and sale readiness. Management succession is the route to remedy this situation.

However, let's be clear: management succession is a journey, not a sprint. It involves upskilling and investing in your team, duplicating costs and time for a period. Yet, at the end of this path, lies a business that doesn't hinge on your presence. Imagine being able to step away for an extended period, knowing the business will continue functioning seamlessly.

As your business evolves, skill gaps will emerge - be it in sales management, financial oversight, or operational leadership. Identifying these gaps is the first step; creating a comprehensive management succession plan is the next. By systematically addressing these gaps, you ensure that your business is not just surviving but thriving, ready for the next phase of its journey.

In conclusion, management succession is not just a business strategy; it's a testament to your business's resilience and its readiness for the future. It's about nurturing future leaders, bridging skill gaps, and reducing the business's dependence on any single individual. Ultimately, it's about crafting a legacy that stands strong even in your absence.

Step 16 – Tax Planning

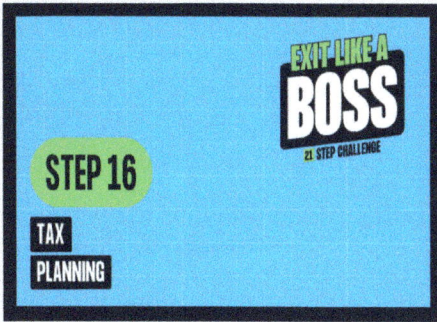

As a business owner preparing to reap the rewards of your hard work and dedication through an exit, the financial landscape can get intricate, especially when it comes to taxes. Here we will tackle the often underestimated but critical aspect of tax planning during the sale of your business.

In numerous jurisdictions, including the majority of countries, selling your business triggers tax implications. These implications may take various forms, such as capital gains tax or income tax, and may vary based on the nature of your sale. However, with meticulous tax planning, you can proactively manage and reduce these tax burdens, staying well within the boundaries of legality and ethical business conduct.

Leveraging Tax Concessions: Insights from Different Regions

Various countries provide specific tax concessions, each tailored to encourage business owners to develop, sell, and fund their retirements. One such example is the small business capital gains tax concessions offered in Australia. These concessions play a pivotal role in minimizing the tax payable upon the sale of a business. To capitalize on these benefits, advanced planning is not just advisable - it's crucial.

Early Birds Get the Tax Benefits

Initiating tax planning well in advance of your planned sale is a strategic decision. Waiting until the eleventh hour might limit your ability to implement effective tax-saving strategies, potentially resulting in higher tax liabilities. Tax planning involves a thorough understanding of the assets being sold, those being retained, and the implications this has on taxation.

A fundamental step is recognizing which assets will be sold and which will be retained, such as business premises or select investments. This choice significantly influences the tax ramifications of your exit. Seeking guidance from tax professionals to comprehend the potential tax costs and how you can minimize them is of paramount importance.

Seeking Wise Counsel: Tax Experts as Your Partners

Engaging experienced tax professionals, be they accountants, tax lawyers, or certified public accountants (CPAs), is a wise move. Their expertise can guide you on structuring the sale, determining the assets to retain, and qualifying for tax concessions. Tax planning should be integrated into your larger exit strategy, seamlessly intertwining with components like business valuation and value optimization.

Aligning with Your Vision: A Comprehensive Approach

Lastly, while considering tax implications, align this with your overarching exit strategy and financial goals. Factor in not only the sale price but also the net proceeds after tax. Modify your plans accordingly to ensure that your exit aligns with your financial objectives.

In summary, understanding and planning for tax implications during the sale of your business is a critical element of exiting successfully. Don't procrastinate - initiate tax planning early, seek professional advice, and strategically navigate the tax landscape. By doing so, you can make the most of your hard-earned business value when the time comes to transition to new endeavors.

Step 17 – Documentation

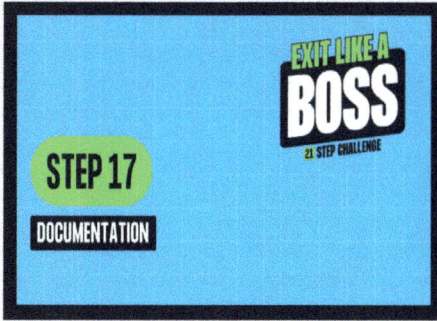

When it comes to selling your small to medium-sized enterprise (SME) business, the journey involves meticulous planning and careful execution. One crucial aspect often overlooked or underestimated is thorough documentation. Here, we will discuss the importance of comprehensive documentation during the selling process and how it can make or break a deal.

The Power of a Well-Crafted Information Memorandum (IM)

An Information Memorandum (IM) is essentially a sales brochure for your business. It provides a comprehensive overview, showcasing your business's history, products, services, market, clientele, and financial performance. A well-structured IM helps potential buyers understand the potential of the business they're considering. Conversely, a poorly written IM can deter potential buyers. Creating an effective IM is vital in presenting your business in the best possible light.

What Should Your IM Include?

A well-rounded IM comprises key information about your business. Start with a historical narrative, detailing the journey of your business, its mission, vision, and core values. Present an in-depth analysis of your product or service, your target market, and your competitive edge.

Financial performance is a crucial section, showcasing your profitability and demonstrating the soundness of your business. It should include revenue, expenses, profits, and any other relevant financial metrics. Include details of any existing contracts or agreements with clients, employment agreements, property leases, and more.

Due Diligence: The Make or Break Moment

The due diligence process is where the deal gets truly serious. Buyers will scrutinize every aspect of your business, making sure the claims made in the IM are accurate and align with reality. It's a comprehensive audit of your business that covers everything from financial records to historical website data and social media engagement.

This process can be extensive and intricate, often spanning 12 to 15 pages of essential items that the buyer needs to review. It's a thorough examination, including everything from the financial statements and tax returns to customer data and website analytics.

Early preparation for due diligence can be a game-changer. Create a repository of all essential documents, contracts, financial records, and other necessary data. This not only streamlines the due diligence process but also presents your business in a favorable light to potential buyers.

Pre-due diligence is a proactive step. Work with professionals to identify gaps or inconsistencies that could be red flags during the due diligence process. By addressing these issues early, you're more likely to instill confidence in potential buyers and ensure a smoother transaction.

Collaborate with Experts

Engage professionals experienced in business transactions, such as CPAs, lawyers, and industry experts, to guide you through the process. Their expertise can be invaluable in helping you compile accurate and comprehensive documentation and ensuring you navigate the sale of your business successfully.

In conclusion, meticulous documentation is not just about presenting your business in the best light; it's about building trust and confidence in potential buyers. It's about ensuring a smooth transaction that is advantageous for both parties involved. Don't underestimate the power of well-crafted documents in securing a successful sale.

Step 18 – Liquidity Event

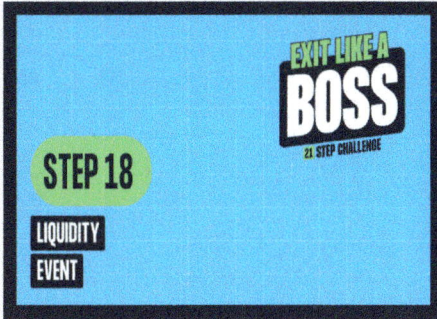

As an SME business owner, the ultimate goal is to maximize the value of your business, especially during a liquidity event - the much-anticipated exit. This is where all the groundwork you've put in, the thorough preparation, finally pays off. However, the key lesson here is not to rush into a sale but to strategically plan and attract the right buyer.

The Strategic Buyer

Not all buyers are created equal, and the difference lies in what they're willing to pay for your business. A typical buyer might offer you two to four times your net profit, but what if you could find a buyer willing to pay six, eight, or even more times the profit? This is where the notion of a strategic buyer comes into play.

A strategic buyer is a buyer who recognizes a unique value in your business that goes beyond the financials. They see potential in your product, service, IP, customer base, or market presence that aligns with their strategic goals. It's not just about selling to anyone but finding the right match.

To find a strategic buyer, you need to understand what makes your business unique and appealing to a certain group. Consider your product, service, IP, market presence, or client profile. Now, think of businesses that have a product or service similar to yours, or would benefit significantly by adding your product or service to their offerings. These are your potential strategic buyers.

Imagine selling laptops and finding a strategic buyer who sells mobile phones. The customers are the same, the buying process is similar, and the strategic value for the buyer is immense.

Leveraging Intangible Assets: A Goldmine for Strategic Buyers

One of the most powerful aspects that can attract a strategic buyer is your intangible assets - intellectual property, unique methods, processes, or recipes. These assets might seem small to you but can be incredibly valuable to a larger player. Consider recipes held by giants like KFC or Coca-Cola. Their strategic value is enormous.

Now, analyze your business. What are your intangible assets? What do you do differently or have that could be highly valuable in the hands of a larger player?

How Listed Companies Transform Valuations

Listed companies are often strategic buyers due to their interest in intangible assets and their higher valuation multiples. They are willing to pay a premium because owning your business could significantly increase their overall valuation. A small to medium business might be valued at two to four times profit, but a listed company could value it at 12 to 13 times profit, creating a substantial opportunity.

Planning Your Strategy for the Liquidity Event

Once you've identified your potential strategic buyers, the next step is to strategize on how to attract them. Showcase the strategic value your business holds for them. Demonstrate how your product or service can seamlessly integrate into their existing portfolio, how it aligns with their long-term goals, and how it can drive their growth and profitability.

As an SME business owner looking to exit with flair, remember that the true essence lies in attracting the right buyer, not just any buyer. Focus on your intangible assets, consider the potential of strategic buyers, and aim for those who see your business as more than just numbers. By doing so, you're not only increasing the potential sale value of your business but also ensuring that your hard work and dedication in building your enterprise pays off in the best possible way.

Step 19 – Investment Planning

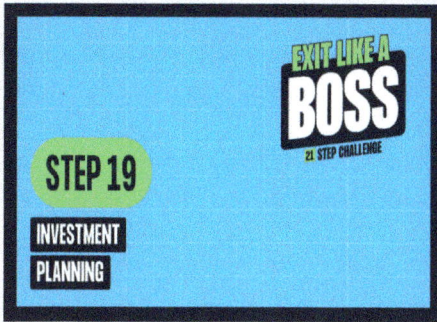

You've made it. You've sold your business, pocketed that hard-earned check, and now you're faced with a new reality. As a business owner, you were accustomed to the ebb and flow of finances, investing in your business when needed and reaping the benefits when possible. But post-exit, this dynamic undergoes a seismic shift. You're no longer pouring money into your business, and it won't be generating income for you either. So, where does your revenue come from now? This is where ongoing investment planning steps in, and it's vital.

Understanding the New Reality

The first thing to recognize is that for the first time, your primary source of income will be your investments. While this is perfectly feasible, it necessitates a shift in mindset and a solid strategy. Previously, the business provided; now, your investments will.

Prolonged Life Expectancy and Increased Spending

Life expectancies have dramatically risen, presenting a unique financial challenge. You may live 20 to 30 years after retiring, meaning you need your finances to last longer than ever. Moreover, post-retirement, having more free time often translates to more spending. Travel, hobbies, and adventures become part of your routine, potentially costing more than your working days.

This brings us back to the importance of setting the right financial goals. Meticulous financial planning ensures you know exactly what you need to fund your retirement. How much do you need from the sale of your business, combined with other assets, to sustain your desired lifestyle?

Seek Professional Guidance

Investment planning at this stage is not a do-it-yourself project. It requires expert guidance. A financial advisor can help you chart a course based on your goals, debt situation, desired lifestyle, and other critical factors. They can help you select appropriate investments and design a strategy that aligns with your vision.

In essence, this underscores the shift from preparing for the exit to navigating life after the sale. Your wealth, once anchored in your business, now sails through the seas of investment. Planning

for these waters requires careful attention and the right guidance to ensure you continue to exit like a boss even after the sale is complete.

Step 20 - Asset Protection

Congratulations, you've successfully exited your business, securing that substantial payout you worked so hard for. Now comes a crucial phase – protecting your newfound assets. No longer can you rely on the constant inflow and outflow of business finances; it's time to ensure your wealth remains intact and secure.

For many entrepreneurs, particularly those of the baby boomer generation, the sale of a business heralds a shift in priorities. Now in your 50s, 60s, or 70s, you've sold your business and received a significant payout. However, the new challenge lies in safeguarding this asset. Unlike before, you can't simply inject more funds or sell another business to recover losses.

The Intricacies of Blended Families

To add to this complexity, many entrepreneurs have blended families, with children from previous marriages or those who've been married and divorced themselves. Navigating this intricate dynamic necessitates a prudent approach to asset protection.

Seeking professional guidance is paramount in this stage. The core of your strategy should focus on understanding what assets you possess and how they are owned or controlled. Utilizing tools like family trusts can offer a robust level of protection. These trusts allow the family to control assets without direct ownership, providing a layer of security.

Assessing Risks and Implementing Safeguards

Now that you've sold your business, your risk profile has changed. Assessing potential risks, such as accidents or lawsuits related to retained assets like a factory or office, becomes essential. Setting up the right legal agreements, insurances, and estate planning measures can go a long way in safeguarding your assets.

Understanding the ownership structure of the assets you choose to retain post-sale is critical. Whether it's a factory, office, or investments, determining the appropriate ownership ensures protection and peace of mind. Consider the lease agreements and who should be the legal owner.

Above all, detailed legal and financial advice should be sought before making decisions on asset protection. Crafting a strategy that aligns with your unique circumstances and family dynamics is key. This ensures that your exit remains a triumph, and your financial gains are secure for the future.

In the end, having exited like a boss, let us not falter in securing what we've gained. With prudent planning and professional guidance, we can fortify our assets and pave the way for a prosperous and secure post-business life.

Step 21 – Estate Planning

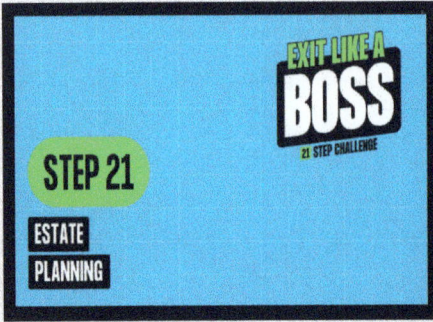

In the exhilarating journey of exiting your business like a boss, we arrive at a topic that might not be at the top of your list: estate planning. Yet, considering the inevitable course of life, it's a critical step that ensures your hard-earned assets find their rightful destinations when you're no longer around. Let's discuss why estate planning is a vital aspect of your exit strategy.

The Inevitability of the Future

No one likes to dwell on the notion of their mortality. However, the truth remains that life follows its course, and we must prepare for the inevitable. Whether it's through passing away or facing a health crisis, we need to ensure our assets are protected and allocated according to our wishes.

Certainty of Outcome

Estate planning offers certainty of outcome. It involves crafting a will and estate planning document that clearly dictates what happens to your assets post your absence. This is particularly crucial if you've used asset protection structures like trusts, super funds, or companies, as it defines how these assets are managed and who benefits from them.

Navigating Modern Challenges

Today, we face additional challenges such as dementia that could render us legally unable to sign a will or estate plan. It's not just about planning for death; it's also about planning for incapacity. This is where powers of attorney come into play, allowing someone else to handle your affairs when you cannot. All these elements – wills, estate plans, powers of attorney – are interconnected and contribute to a comprehensive strategy.

Learning from Past Mistakes

We can draw valuable lessons from unfortunate instances where proper estate planning was overlooked. Imagine having successfully sold your business, receiving a substantial payout, but failing to formalize your estate plan. In a tragic twist of fate, an unforeseen accident claims you. The absence of a will and estate plan leaves your family in a legal and financial predicament, overshadowing an already tragic event.

Given these possibilities, the urgency to draft a solid estate plan cannot be overstated. Seek the expertise of financial advisors and lawyers to guide you through this process. It might involve several steps and a plethora of documents, but the peace of mind knowing that your loved ones are protected and provided for is priceless.

Continuing the 'Exit Like a Boss' Journey

Exiting your business isn't a conclusion, but a transition to the next chapter. It's about securing your legacy, ensuring that the wealth you've accumulated enriches the lives of your family and supports causes close to your heart. The journey continues, and estate planning is a pivotal part of it.

In conclusion, embrace estate planning as a responsible and forward-thinking business owner. It's a way to protect and provide for your loved ones, preserving the legacy you've worked so hard to build. The essence of exiting like a boss extends beyond the sale – it's about securing your legacy and ensuring a bright future for those you care about.